HEALING IN GOD'S POWER

POETRY BY YVONNE GREEN

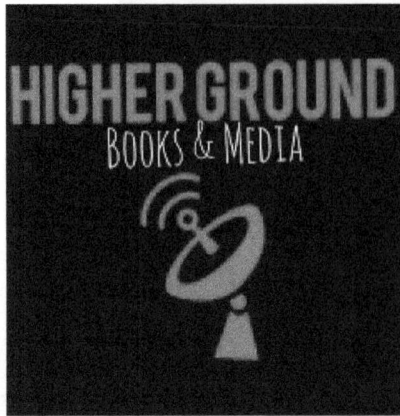

Scripture taken from the HOLY BIBLE, NEW INTERNATIONAL VERSION®. NIV®. Copyright © 1973, 1978, 1984 by International Bible Society. Used by permission of Zondervan. All rights reserved worldwide.

Higher Ground Books & Media
Springfield, Ohio.
http://highergroundbooksandmedia.com

Printed in the United States of America 2019

HEALING IN GOD'S POWER

POETRY BY YVONNE GREEN

Introduction

The words written in this book are heartfelt. Some of my deepest darkest feelings are written on these pages. I wear my heart on my sleeve. It is important to have an outlet. Holding things in is not good for our mental health and well-being. In life we have to remember we are in charge of our own happiness. Giving myself to the Lord is one of the best things that ever happened to me. If it had not been for the Lord, where would I be? Just believe all things are possible, just take the steps, keep God first, pray and most importantly believe.

Minister Yvonne Green

The foundational Scripture for this book is Jeremiah 29:11 which says, "'For I know the plans I have for you,' declares the Lord, 'plans to prosper you and not to harm you, plans to give you hope and a future.'"

Dedications & Acknowledgements

First, I want to give God the Glory for He is the head of my life. I want to dedicate this first book to the following;

Betty Jones-Mom

Elisha Reynolds -Dad

I want to thank my parents for their love, support and understanding. I can never repay them for all they have done.

Donald Jones-Step Dad- who was called home Feb 2009. He was the one who encouraged me to write a poetry book.

Kanisa Reynolds-Daughter

Dontae Reynolds-Son

Jamal Reynolds- Son

To my children you three were the spark that kept me going. Thank you, I love you very much.

Zoe Reynolds

Andrew McKnight

Kaylen McKnight

Zander McKnight

Ava Lowe

Alivia – Mentee

Pastor Moses Peterson Jr.-Uplift Ministries thank you for teaching me, giving me wisdom and knowledge.

Special dedication to Sister Rebecca Benston for helping me publish my first book.

This book is also dedicated to all my family, and my dearest closest friends. There are so many Pastors and Ministers in the city of Springfield who have helped make an impact in my life and who has helped me. Thank you, Pastor Cornelius Hookfin for allowing me to have a venue to do community events. Pastor Grayson as the coordinator many years ago for Save Our Young People as well as the Save Our Young People committee. Thank you to all the advocates, and leaders in our community who led the way for me. Thank you to all who have encouraged, inspired and prayed for me over the years. I truly appreciate all of you. I would not be the woman I am today without many of you, there are too many to name, but all of you have made a difference in my life. I am so grateful. God bless you all.

Untitled

Too many thoughts gathered in my mind.

Asking and questioning God when is my due time....

To receive all you have promised me.

My naked eyes cannot see the blessings that await in the midst of captivity.

Or do I see the negativity the enemy is throwing swiftly, as far as can be.

Pick me up God, restore and rebuild the hope, dream and reality that is within me.

That seems to be broken down into fragments, due to resilience and resistance.

The enemy cannot dictate the outcome of my delivery.

Because God has already told me, there is Glory through the suffering of my story.

My Testimony

My Testimony was a journey just for me, you see.

A journey God had to walk me through, to show me,

there is light at the end of the tunnel.

Sometimes, I would wonder why, as tears rolled down my weeping eyes.

God said, Trust me, my child.

The very thing you preach, the very thing you teach,

as you walk through the water, as you walk through the fire,

I was there when no one cared.

Trust in all things, because I was there,

as you bear witness and confess a scorned heart.

My child, I knew you from the start.

For all the sisters and brothers,

the test became testimony to reach others.

As hard and unbearable as it may have seemed,

the vision my child, was beyond reality.

Filled with Emotions

I do not even know where to begin.

Sharing my hurts, disappointments and pain.

No longer can I pretend. So many emotions intertwined inside,

a fragment portion no longer can I hide.

The rawness and burning desires in my heart which was filled

with love and compassion, from the very start.

Balled up like a fetus inside the womb, anger festering,

Sheltering like the butterfly inside the cocoon.

If it was not for the Lord, where would I be?

A prisoner with shackles, isolated without the key.

Brokenness

Brokenness is what I feel inside this, I can confide.

My heart cannot believe the feelings and loss of reality.

Trying to grasp hold of all the desires of my heart, but

you were broken as well, from the very start.

You never truly received the gift God placed within thee.

Do you have a clue, the brokenness in you?

The things broken, only God can heal, time cannot be still.

Brokenness will continue to fester.

Two broken hearts that have died, bleeding, cold, and withered inside.

The brokenness is real.

Reclaim Our City

A city lost and out of control.

Violence and murders at an all-time high.

Genocide of a generation.

Vigils and funerals wall to wall.

Through tragedy, lives being saved through the alter call.

Others ready to point fingers, accusations of stealing visions.

When in reality the spotlight is not about us, but the kingdom.

So let the sirens come.

The cycle will never end, for as the Bible says, we are living in the last days.

We need to love one another, in Gods eyes we are all sisters and brothers.

There is no time to argue and no time to fight.

We shall proclaim the victory when we come together to reclaim this city.

My Dear Lady

The bruises you can attempt to conceal.

You cannot hide, the abuse is obvious you see.

The demeanor on your face displays fear within thee.

My dear lady, you are not a punching bag, no matter how mad he gets.

My dear lady you are more precious than silver and gold.

You are a child of the most high, truth be told.

Get out while you can, before it is too late.

Do not seal your own fate.

God has a hold of you and will give you strength to go on alone.

My dear lady this abuse you can no longer condone.

Healing in God's Purpose

The growth within me, came from suffering and pain.

Unbearable at times, I felt I was going insane.

Through God's mercy and grace, it was his love and power

that put this smile upon my face.

For God knew the plans for my life.

Happiness combined with heartache and strife.

The trials, transgressions and sin were within.

We all have to be a testimony for those living in darkness

and the light for others to see.

There is healing in God's purpose

if you just believe.

You are my light, you are my life!

My life, I'm overseeing, my joy, my every being.

Can you see, you are a part of me? You are my kids,

you are my sight, guiding me to the light of the world that's

so dark. You are my inspiration, you are my soul, my will to

keep going, as my evolutions unfold. Do not underestimate

your purpose, your fate, your existence in my very life.

You gave me power to override such physical strife, with my

unconditional love, and blessings continue to simmer from the

Almighty Father above.

Hurtful memories, time to erase

A little girl grew up to be insecure.
What was the reason for the sadness in her world, who knows?
Just a typical teen trying to fit on the scene.
Words can never hurt me, that's one big lie, you see.
For I was tortured with names, this is no mind game.
Ridiculed by one soul, it was not funny, it was out of control.
I know beauty is on the inside as well as out.
Focus in the mirror, see what admirers are talking about.
I know now, others don't determine who you are, for I am loved by God thus far.
I learned I am loved by my parents, kids, family and friends.
Now learning to love thyself within.
Just know beauty is in the eye of the beholder, for ladies we laugh while crying on each other's shoulders.
I am a child of God, he makes no mistakes this is one topic you don't need to debate.
For I bow to my Father above who praises me with his unconditional love.
You don't have to have drop dead gorgeous looks or look like models in the fashion books.
For I know beauty from the start.
I know I have a philosophical compassionate heart sparkles in the eye.
Such sweet whispers leave tears as I cry for the joy I embrace.
Hurtful memories, I now will erase, and forgive thee, for God forgave me.

Give Myself Away

I accept my calling on this July 17 day.

I accept my calling, totally giving myself away.

I perceived being called by the Holy Spirit.

The urge was persistent, I no longer could resist.

I tried for a few days to hide, but within me, Jesus,

the Son of God, the Holy Spirit resides.

How must I repay thee, serving for my Lord, abundantly?

Use me Lord, use me in your way

Use me Lord, guide me in the things I say.

Take me by the hand, give me everlasting strength to stand.

Have your way with me, so others can see,

even when you're lost and misbehave,

God loves you unconditionally.

You can still be saved.

There is abundance of blessings coming your way.

Just be obedient in the things that he says.

I love you all.

Come one, come all, even though you misbehaved.

Jesus says, come to me and you shall be saved.

The Battle has Just Begun

The battle has just begun.

Day by day, one by one.

You see God made plans for my life, even before I was born.

No matter what you do to try to destroy me,

my life will not be scorned.

I will not give you the satisfaction of destroying me.

I am a mighty child of God, you see.

You are the predator ready to devour.

I am protected by my Father

and his mighty sword even to my final hour.

So devil, I do not care if you hate me.

I will never bow down to your level you see.

Whatever you bring my way, I'm ready to fight,

claiming my victory every day.

My battle has begun, so don't think I will lie down.

Do you think you have won?

I'm not gonna give up, I'm not gonna go insane.

I will always praise forever, in Jesus name.

A Strong Black Woman

I could never have a heart of steel,
I feel with every intense desire.
I wish not to be mediocre, I want to strive higher.
I am a woman. A strong black woman.
My traits are underneath my skin. Truly within.
My heart and compassion was passed on to me, you see.
From my Mother, what a wonderful human being.
Beautiful, compassionate, strong and bold, her true qualities
and a heart of gold. This woman had sacrificed so much for
me in her life, despite any heartache, sorrow and strife. Every
barrier that was thrown her way, she conquered, and still
maintains her dignity to this day.
A woman, a strong black woman, living her life to the fullest.
No judgement from her I must confess. A woman, a strong
woman. I thank God, for this blessing. Unthinkable, that I
could be a replica to her in many ways, while being humble,
that is the key. I think a lot of people would agree, to seeing
not only a woman, but a strong black woman in me.

Don't You See!

For a moment in time, just sit back and let this marinate in your mind.

Joyous and happy as can be.

Now torn down insecure and self-conscious as can be.

Your eyes use to glisten so bright.

Now your eyes are startled like a deer in front of headlights!

What happened to the sweet spirit within?

A soul that is now lost trying to conform to the image of her mate and friends.

Listen, be who God created you to be.

If you're trying to please others, you're not being true to yourself!

Don't you see?

Tears you cry

I see the tears you cry!

I know you wonder why.

You were on cloud nine and everything seemed perfectly fine.

Then all of a sudden, an outpour,

a chilling feeling you try to hide!

You try to quench the spirit.

No longer can you hide!

All the hurt and pain you have endured for a while.

No one can never truly know what hides behind a smile!

How many more heartaches can you bare?

Sometimes one may feel as if God is not on your side.

This truth I must confide.

God is with you, God is near,

God is not the author of your worries and fears!

Every person he has brought in your life.

Every person that has caused you heartache and strife

is part of the master plan.

God has helped you take a stand!

He wants you to be happy!

A life full of peace.

Rid all anger, heartache, bitterness, it's time to cease.

It's time you take control of being the best you can be.

Being the best man or woman that God has chosen you to be!

All things are possible

Trust God, even when we don't understand.

We have to trust even when we can't comprehend.

God has plans for our lives, but we often steer to the left, and

our plans do not coincide.

We have to pray, each and every day.

Pray about guidance and direction.

Pray about important decisions, to have confirmation about

our visions.

We have to pray and trust God in good times and bad.

Pray when we are happy and when we are sad.

At times our faith may waiver, but with God's favor nothing is

totally impossible.

With God, all things are possible.

We don't have to serve a lifetime sentence for a past God has forgave us for.

We can heal

Lies filthiness, discontentment, broken hearts, anger and a lot of resentment.

Our past does not define us, at last we can define our past.

This bulletin just in, "God forgave us for our sins."

It is important in life to forgive others as well as ourselves.

We have all been lost at a point where we needed help.

It is time to move forward once and for all, to hold our heads up and walk tall.

There is no need to be phony, if it was not for our testimony where would we be?

You see our testimony encourages others.

Our testimony gives light to our sisters and brothers.

Let's start today, be positive in all ways.

Let's not be at a standstill.

We have to let God rebuild us so we can truly heal.

Trying to hide what we feel inside

Often in life, it's hard to articulate the incredible painful

moments of silence.

As if we are totally insane.

Trying to hide what we really feel inside.

Loneliness often concealed with a smile.

We never confess how broken we truly are.

Prisoners of our own will, image killed and ready to seal the

deal.

Holding ourselves hostage to our past, feelings of

unworthiness that seldom fade and often last.

Rise above it all, because our Lord and Savior is here to catch

us when we fall.

Untitled

Do we truly understand what is happening in our lives?

Sometimes filled with so much pain, agony and strife.

What do we do when we want to give in?

When we act as if everything is fine, we often pretend.

Pretty faces often tell lies, not living but merely existing.

No one knows what lies behind a smile, bondage, brokenness, resentment, everything compiled.

Through it all, there is one we can call, our heavenly father above,

who will rebuild us with his unconditional love.

Untitled

Things will work in our favor if we just believe, we shall receive.

We shall receive the blessings God has bestowed upon our lives, but it won't come overnight.

Do not put trust in man, but realize God will show us the plan.

This is no game, but he does not disclose the time frame.

Sometimes it may be hard to wait, not knowing the date.

We have to be patient, in all things.

And believe our Lord and Savior is the king.

No matter how hard it gets, we have to believe in every endeavor, things will work in our favor.

I will overcome this pain.

I know life can be rough and at times I feel like giving up.
I know life can be rough and at times I feel like giving up.
I will, I shall, I will overcome this pain.
I will, I shall, I will overcome this pain.

Lord, please heal me,
Lord please cleanse me.
Lord please restore me.
Lord please forgive me.

Life is overwhelming me,
Lord please help me.
Lord please don't forget me.
Lord I just want to be happy.
Lord please uplift me.
Lord please forgive my travesties.
Lord please don't ever leave me.
Lord please help me.
Lord please rebuild me.
Lord please deliver me.
Lord please teach me Lord please mold me.
Lord help me see the blessing.
Lord please empty me.
Lord please help me be the best I can be.
Lord please use me.
Lord please save me.
Lord please hear me.
Lord please use me.

I will, I shall, I will overcome this pain.

A woman's worth

Embrace our beauty, we have to embrace our skin.

We must treasure the woman within.

You see, we have to be the women God created us to be.

We have to be original, be unique, humble, this is no time to

compete.

There is no time for jealousy.

Loving who we are is the simple key.

Let us not settle for less, in God's eyes we deserve the best.

Now is the time to break the curse, it is well beyond time to

recognize a woman's worth.

Bring Awareness

One never knows what lies behind a smile.

We have to check on friends we have not heard from in a while.

Isolation, Depression, Suicide, Ideation is just a few.

This topic is a hush hush discussion, but it is something we must do.

To bring awareness to the deep dark suppression.

To those who have lost their way, please get up, seek help to face these days.

Do not listen to the devil and his lies, he is out to seek, conquer, destroy and demise.

God is there, he truly cares when you are sad and feeling blue.

Remember, God is there to carry you.

A world divided

What a sad display.

Hatred, racism, bigotry and the prejudice we are witnessing

today.

This should not be,

is this truly our reality?

To hate because of the color of our skin.

I cannot comprehend the cruel, dark ways,

the things people do,

the things people say.

God is love and it is important we live in peace.

Let's get back to loving one another,

for in God's eyes we are all sisters and brothers.

Live life

Life is short and tomorrow is not guaranteed for you or for me.

Let us live today as if it's our last.

Let us be joyful and happy, because life on earth slips away fast.

Many of us exist but do not live.

Let us be free, let us learn to forgive.

When we hold onto unforgiveness it steals our peace.

It is time to bury the hatchet so the anger can cease.

Let us love the life we live and live the life we love.

While praising our heavenly father looking down on us from above.

If my people

Shots blast all through the night.

Shortly, after we hear Care flight.

God please, no more fatalities.

No more young people, no more casualties.

We quickly jump on Facebook to look.

So much pity, 2018 fourteen murders in our city.

Parents losing children, children losing parents.

Retaliation methodology with so much resentment.

When will the cycle end?

If my people can see, we can no longer pretend.

Realize churches can no longer hide,

it is time we all come together and put our differences aside.

Time to rise

Take a chance and praise God in advance.

Let us stop stressing and celebrate the blessings.

Let go of strife and thank God for our life.

Life can sometimes be a struggle, we must not give up.

Let us jump the hurdle.

The current situation is not the final destination.

Let us be victorious and not victims.

There is so much drama our lives sometimes feel like a

sitcom.

It is time to rise above it all, because God will surely catch us if

we take a fall.

I had to go

In order to grow I had to go.

No, it was not me who left, but God who sent me away.

God says to grow, to develop,

To mature me, in so many ways.

I learned to endure. I learned how to prepare.

I learned how to push, press and persevere.

Not too sure what I would do without you.

I would not have had the experience to advance my

knowledge or share wisdom.

To further prepare me for spreading good news in the

kingdom.

Now I know in order to grow, I had to go.

Rejected but Protected

Often in life we may be rejected, but we have to realize it is for our protection.

We may not understand at the present time.

We feel sad, dismayed, cry and whine.

But this you can bet, Gods no often means a better yes.

We may not understand or comprehend Gods plan for our life.

So do not feel unworthy, and please do not be in a hurry.

Unwind because God will say Yes in his precise due time.

About the Author

Yvonne Green is a compassionate woman of God who loves giving back to her community. She is a Minister/Evangelist/Prayer Warrior who loves to encourage others and minister to youth and young adults. Yvonne accepted her calling to minister in July of 2011and preached her first sermon on March 14, 2012 under the leadership of Pastor Larry D Coleman at Restored Life Ministries and she has been on fire for the Lord ever since. Yvonne firmly believes we are in control of our own happiness. She believes failure only leads to the road to success. Yvonne's favorite mottos are, "Give loved one's flowers while here on Earth," "Do not be a carbon copy, be original and unique," and "We have to be the person God created us to be." Yvonne lives in Springfield, Ohio.

Other titles from Higher Ground Books & Media:

Wise Up to Rise Up by Rebecca Benston

A Path to Shalom by Steen Burke

Overcomer by Forrest Henslee

Miracles: I Love Them by Forest Godin

I Don't Want to Be Like You by Maryanne Christiano-Mistretta

32 Days with Christ's Passion by Mark Etter

Knowing Affliction and Doing Recovery by John Baldasare

Out of Darkness by Stephen Bowman

The Tin Can Gang by Chuck David

Whobert the Owl by Mya C. Benston

Anomaly by Derra Nicole Sabo

Jack Kramer's Journey by Frank Adkins

Man Made by Grace by Willie White

For His Eyes Only by John Salmon

Add these titles to your collection today!

http://highergroundbooksandmedia.com

www.ingramcontent.com/pod-product-compliance
Lightning Source LLC
Chambersburg PA
CBHW021922040426
42448CB00007B/863